CW00758898

RUDE COCKTAILS

Written and compiled by Paul Wilcox

KUDOS

Published by Kudos, an imprint of Top That! Publishing plc.

Tide Mill Way, Woodbridge, Suffolk, IP12 1AP.
www.kudosbooks.com

Contents

Introduction

Ready for an Angel's Kiss, or how about a Comfortable Screw after a memorable encounter with a Horny Bull? It may sound like dirty talk but this book is all about seriously sexy cocktails – what you do after drinking them is entirely up to you!

Use the rudeness rating to select from old favourites such as a Harvey Wallbanger or why not pick some more unusual drinks to impress your nearest and dearest.

Armed with this book and just a few spirits and mixers, you'll soon be the image of style and sophistication – so prepare to impress!

To make life a little easier there's a handy reference section that will give you an idea of what all the spirits and syrups taste like. There are also tips on equipment and techniques, so shake that booty and stir it up with some rude, but oh so sophisticated, cocktails!

Note: Cocktail photographs may feature larger measures than stated. However, it is NOT recommended that you exceed the given amounts. This publication endorses responsible drinking.

The Booze...

Amaretto – An Italian liqueur with a nutty, almond flavour.

Brandy – Any spirit distilled from fermented fruit juice is a brandy. It is most commonly a golden-colour spirit distilled from grapes.

Coffee liqueur – The most common brand comes from Mexico and is flavoured with coffee beans and brandy.

Crème de Banane – Strong smelling banana liqueur.

Crème de Cacao – Very sweet, cocoa and vanilla flavoured liqueur.

Crème de Framboise – Delicately flavoured raspberry liqueur.

Curaçao – Sweet, orange flavoured liqueur widely used in cocktails.

Galliano – An Italian liqueur flavoured with herbs.

Gin – Spirit flavoured with juniper berries. Sloe gin is flavoured with sloe berries.

Grenadine – Pomegranate flavoured sugar syrup. Non-alcoholic but an essential for cocktails.

Irish Cream – This is a liquer mainly made from a blend of Irish cream and Irish whisky.

Orange liqueur – As the name suggests, an orange flavoured liqueur from France.

Rum – Spirit distilled from molasses. Rum varies in quality and colour.

Sambuca – A clear Italian spirit flavoured with aniseed.

Schnapps – A Dutch or German spirit normally distilled from potatoes in a variety of fruit flavours.

Tequila – A spirit distilled in Mexico from an agave plant.

Triple Sec – Very dry, colourless curaçao.

Vodka – Essential for cocktails. Distilled grain spirit.

Whisky – Fermented cereals form the base for this spirit. Bourbon is a type of whisky made from maize.

As a general note, the standard measures for spirits are 25 ml (single) or 50 ml (double). Cocktail measures often given in multiples of 15 ml.

...and the Moves

Glasses:

Cocktail – Triangular glass on a stem. A cocktail glass is used for short strong drinks, such as a dry Martini. The stem ensures your hand doesn't warm the drink.

Highball – Tall, straight sided glass for 'long' drinks. The tallest version is a Collins.

Pilsner – Tall 'V' shaped glass for long drinks or beer.

Shot – Used for short spirits without ice.

Tumbler – Also known as a 'rocks' glass. Often used for spirits or drinks served 'on the rocks'.

Techniques:

Blend – Place all ingredients including crushed ice in a blender and blend until smooth.

Build – Pour ingredients into the glass one on top of the other.

Crushing ice – Ice must be crushed before putting it in a blender, and some cocktails can be served with crushed ice. Wrap the ice in a clean tea towel to crush and use as required.

Float – Pour the liquid very slowly over the back of a spoon so it floats on the top.

Frost – To frost a glass, rub lemon juice around the rim before dipping into salt or sugar. Using orange juice or grenadine will give a coloured rim.

Shake – Put the ingredients into a cocktail shaker, including ice if specified, and shake. A short up and down action is best. Then strain the drink into the glass straight away before the ice dilutes it.

Stir – Pour the ingredients into a mixing glass with ice, stir and strain into the glass.

Twist – Use a small piece of fruit peel and twist it until a few drops of the oil drop into the drink. It is usual to drop the peel into the drink as well.

Glass ....Cocktail

Garnish ....Nutmeg

Rudeness 1

Angel's **Kiss**

Pucker up and prepare for the sweet taste of an angel's kiss.

Ingredients

30 ml vodka
15 ml white crème de cacao
30 ml apple schnapps
15 ml single cream
nutmeg

Method

Frost the rim of the glass with nutmeg. Shake all the ingredients with ice and strain into the glass. Sprinkle more nutmeg on top.

Glass ....Highball

Garnish............A slice of orange

Rudeness..................5

Bend-Me-Over

A dangerous 'pro-position'.

Ingredients

25 ml vodka
25 ml amaretto
Add orange juice to taste

Method

Serve with ice and build ingredients over the top. Garnish with a slice of orange.

Glass ....Cocktail

Garnish.........Strips of lemon zest

Rudeness 4

Between the Sheets

A great way to impress your partner outside the real bed sheets.

Ingredients

30 ml orange liqueur
30 ml brandy
30 ml white rum
15 ml lemon juice

Method

Shake all ingredients with ice and strain into the glass. Serve with a twist of lemon.

Glass ....Cocktail

Garnish ....Sugar frosted rim, umbrella

Rudeness..................3

Climax

The perfect end to a romantic evening.

Ingredients

15 ml vodka
15 ml amaretto
15 ml triple sec
15 ml crème de cacao
15 ml crème de banane

Method

Frost the rim of the glass with sugar. Shake with ice, strain into a cocktail glass and serve.

Glass ....Highball

Garnish.............Slices of orange, lemon & lime

Rudeness..................3

Comfortable Screw

Simple, but something you'll want to enjoy again and again.

Ingredients

50 ml vodka
25 ml bourbon
60 ml orange juice

Method

Pour ingredients into a glass and stir. Served with plenty of ice.

Glass ....Cocktail

Garnish ....Umbrella

Rudeness 2

French Kiss

Oh-la-la – indeed.

Ingredients

50 ml vodka
45 ml crème de framboise
20 ml white crème de cacao
20 ml single cream

Method

Shake all the ingredients together with ice and strain into a glass.

Glass .... Tumbler

Garnish .... A slice of orange

Rudeness 1

Fuzzy Navel

Simple, but you may feel a bit fuzzy after a few of these!

Ingredients

50 ml peach schnapps
orange juice

Method

Put ice into a glass and pour in the schnapps. Top up with orange juice.

Glass ....Highball

Garnish.........Slices of orange & lime

Rudeness..................4

Slow Comfortable Screw

Definitely something to savour.

Ingredients

25 ml vodka
25 ml sloe gin
25 ml bourbon or whisky
orange juice

Method

Shake the first three ingredients with ice. Strain into the glass with ice and top up with orange juice.

Glass ....Highball

Garnish......Pineapple & orange wedges

Rudeness..................4

Hawaiian Screw

Try this for a fruity and exotic path to fulfilment.

Ingredients

60 ml vodka
50–75 ml orange juice
50–75 ml pineapple juice

Method

Serve over ice. Garnish with a wedge of pineapple and orange on the side of the glass.

Glass............Tumbler

Garnish...........A slice of lime

Rudeness.................5

Screaming Orgasm

Give your partner a treat they're sure to remember!

Ingredients

25 ml vodka
25 ml Irish cream liqueur
25 ml coffee flavoured liqueur

Method

Stir ingredients with ice and pour into a tumbler over fresh ice.

Glass ....Highball

Garnish ....A slice of orange, foil pick

Rudeness 4

Indecent Proposal

I'll show you mine if you show me yours.

Ingredients

25 ml white rum
25 ml coconut flavoured white rum
15 ml grenadine
orange juice

Method

Build the spirits and grenadine in the glass. Top up with orange juice and serve with ice.

Glass..............Tumbler

Garnish........Foil pick

Rudeness...................4

Orgasm

Warm, satisfying – and a very tasty drink too.

Ingredients

30 ml orange liqueur
30 ml Irish cream liqueur

Method

Pour the two ingredients over ice and serve.

Glass ....Highball

Garnish.......A slice of orange, cherries

Rudeness..................2

Horny Bull

A matador and a bull-ring may be required.

Ingredients

45 ml tequila
15 ml grenadine
100 ml orange juice
30 ml lemonade

Method

Blend with crushed ice. Serve in a highball glass with an orange wedge.

Glass...............Pilsner

Garnish............A slice of orange

Rudeness..................4

Sex on the Beach

An exotic taste to remind you of a special holiday.

Ingredients

25 ml vodka
25 ml peach schnapps
150 – 200 ml cranberry juice
50 – 100 ml orange juice

Method

Shake ingredients with ice and strain into a pilsner glass. Serve with ice and a slice of orange.

Glass............Tumbler

Garnish...........A slice of orange

Rudeness.................3

Sex on the Sofa

For the perfect way to spend a night in.

Ingredients

45 ml vodka
20 ml peach schnapps
45 ml orange juice
45 ml cranberry juice

Method

Shake all the ingredients with ice and strain into glass over fresh ice.

00.00.04
00.00.05

Glass ....Cocktail

Garnish ....Umbrella

Rudeness 2

Silk Panty

Smooth, alluring and sure to be enjoyed by both of you.

Ingredients

30 ml peach schnapps
30 ml vodka
50 ml cranberry juice

Method

Shake ingredients together with ice and serve in a chilled glass with fresh ice.

Glass.............Tumbler

Garnish.......A slice of orange, foil picks

Rudeness..................5

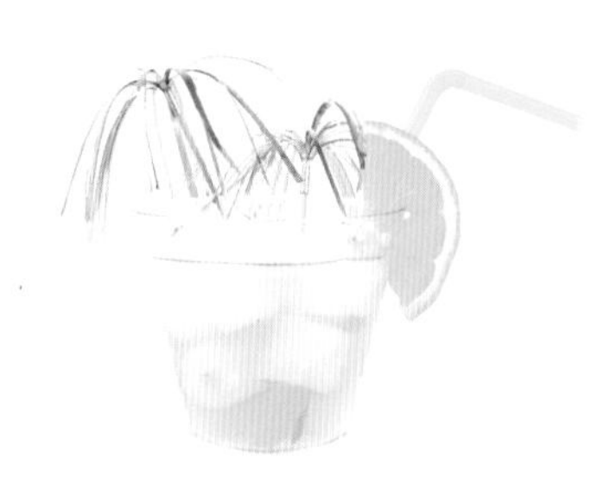

Slippery Dick

One that slips down very nicely.

Ingredients

45 ml gin
Splash of cognac-based, orange flavoured liqueur

Method

Shake with ice. Serve with ice in a tumbler, or strain into a chilled tumbler.

Glass.....................Shot

Garnish.........A cherry

Rudeness...................2

Slippery Nipple

A firm but steady grip comes in useful when handling this cocktail.

Ingredients

25 ml Irish cream liqueur
25 ml sambuca

Method

Float sambuca over Irish cream liqueur in equal measures. Balance a speared cherry on top.

Glass .... Pilsner

Garnish .... Slices of orange

Rudeness 3

Harvey Wallbanger

You'll have a banging time with this one!

Ingredients

60 ml vodka
25 ml galliano
100–125 ml orange juice

Method

Add the vodka and orange juice to a glass and stir. Float the galliano on top. Garnish with a slice of orange.

Glass.....Whatever you fancy. This recipe will make a good jugful.

Rudeness...................5

Why don't we get Drunk and Screw?

Make a statement your partner's sure to understand.

Ingredients

568 ml (1 pint) cherry brandy
325 ml rum
300 ml orange juice
soda water

Method

Mix all the ingredients except the soda water in a large jug, with crushed ice. Add soda water to taste.

Conclusion

This book will have provided you with enough knowledge to create the perfect cocktail for any romantic occasion. Perhaps you've enjoyed the taste of a Slippery Nipple, or maybe you experienced Sex on the Sofa followed by a Screaming Orgasm…? Whatever your choice of cocktail, you're sure to have had a slinky and sexy evening!